THE

BEAGLE

THE BALD BEAGLE

Nature-ly Funny Jokes and Riddles

**by Ferida Wolff
and Dolores Kozielski**

illustrated by Dan Piraro

ISBN 0-590-97496-3

Copyright © 1996 by Ferida Wolff & Dolores Kozielski.
TRUMPET and the TRUMPET logo are registered trademarks of Scholastic Inc. All rights reserved. Published by Scholastic Inc.

12 11 10 9 8 7 6 5 4 3 2 1   6 7 8 9/9 0 1/0

Printed in the U.S.A.

For Aunt Libby,
who loves to laugh

—FW

For Aunt Edith,
with love

—DK

CONTENTS

HORSING AROUND

DALE: What animal likes to go to yard sales?
EVAN: The yaardvark.

What does a mouse weigh on a cat's scale?
About three pounces.

What goat doesn't have any parents?
Little Orphan Nanny.

How do pigs talk to each other?
In swine language.

A book never written:
Dining on Leftovers
by Ali and Tom Katz

Who eats tin cans and picks on kids smaller than himself?
The bully goat.

What does a sheep put on her eyes to protect them from the sun?
Lambshades.

ROY: Roger, why didn't your horse finish the race?
ROGER: Because he got colt feet.

On what holiday do pigs get dressed up?
Gown Hog's Day.

What sound comes from a pigpen?
Ink, ink, ink.

A book never written:
When to Butt in
by Bill E. Goat

Who doesn't have any hair and thinks he's the national dog of the United States?
The bald beagle.

Cow ward: A hospital room for frightened cattle.

What animal enlisted in the military?
The armydillo.

**When Daddy Buffalo leaves for work,
what does he say to his little boy?**
"Bye, son."

Where do sheep go for a haircut?
To the baa baa shop.

**Why won't the other jungle cats play
with the spotted cat?**
Because he's a cheetah.

What's the difference between a dromedary's floor cleaner and Moby Dick in a police hat?

One is a camel mop and the other is a mammal cop.

How do you keep an elephant in the yard?
Put up an ele-fence.

Knock, knock.
Who's there?
Cajun.
Cajun who?
Cajun a mountain lion is dangerous work.

A book never written:
Trapped by a Bear
by Iwanda Gohome

What did Mother Lion give to her young lions for dessert?
Cubcakes.

How does a pig eat?
With its pork chops.

What do you get when you cross a question mark with a two-ton, one-horned animal?
A why–nocerous.

Why was the bear shedding so much?
Because he rubbed against a fir tree.

DON'T BUG ME

Why is a caterpillar able to wait patiently in her cocoon?
Because she knows that she'll be out in a moth or so.

What do bees wear when they go swimming?
Their bee-kinis.

What kind of ceremony do spiders have when they decide to get married?
A webbing.

What do you call a black and yellow insect that doesn't know how to use its stinger?
A bumbling idiot.

A book never written:
Out for Blood
by Moe Squito

Who crawls, has 100 legs, and says "Ho, ho, ho?"
Santapede.

What bugs run away from home?
Fleas.

What's delivered every day to a fly's house?
The fly paper.

Where do flies take their dirty laundry?
To the fly cleaners.

What animal and insect should you take on a hot-air balloon ride?
The high-ena and the low-cust.

Which insect is old and lives inside a tall timepiece?
The grandfather clock-roach.

A book never written:
Termites in the House
by A. Woody Mess

Score-pion: A point keeper at a southwestern basketball game.

What bug has a stormy personality?
The thunder and lightning bug.

Fly squatter: A crouching insect.

Knock, knock.
Who's there?
Virus.
Virus who?
Vi Russ is sick, I'll never know.

Why are ants always getting cut?
Because they crawl on blades of grass.

Prying mantis: A busybody insect.

What do you call an ant's long-eared stuffed toy?
Bug's Bunny.

FIRST BEE: Did you hear about the queen's allergies?
SECOND BEE: No, what happened?
FIRST BEE: She broke out in hives.

Why was the mouse afraid to go to the circus?
Because he might have to sit near the trap-eze.

Lady bug: A listening device for women.

SKY HIGH

Why was the duck kicked out of his apartment?
Because he put too many quacks in the walls.

Why did the farmer put a chicken over the fireplace?
Because he wanted a mantel cluck.

A book never written:
Dress Yourself in Pink
by Flo Mingo

How do chickens save money when they shop?
They use their coop-ons.

Why is an owl such a busybody?
He always wants to know "Who? Who?"

What tool does the blackbird use to change a flat tire?
He uses his crowbar.

What does Daddy Rooster say to Baby Rooster when he misbehaves?
Oh, crow up!

What bird rings your doorbell, then circles your house?
The buzzard.

What kind of bird bowls well?
The spare-row.

What did the pigeon say when he scratched his feathers?
Itchy, itchy, coo.

JOAN: Have you seen the new play about Edgar Allan Poe?
STEVE: No. Is it good?
JOAN: I give it a raven review.

What's round and black, slides on ice, and says "Quack, quack?"
A hockey duck.

A book never written:
How to Hatch a Dinosaur Egg
by Terry Dactyl

What bird is good at choosing the right furniture?
The woodpicker.

Condorminium: An apartment building owned by birds of prey.

What did Mother Hen feed to Baby Hen?
Chick-peas.

Knock, knock.
Who's there?
Tweet.
Tweet who?
Tweet me nicely and I'll be nice to you.

**Who has a badge and spreads his
feathers when he yells "Stick 'em up?"**
The peacop.

DUMMY: If you're so smart, tell me how to
separate lovebirds.
BRAIN: Sure. Put them in an apart-ment
house.

What's the difference between an owl's timepiece and a mixed-up sentence?
One is a bird watch and the other is a word botch.

Which bird loves whipped cream pastries?
The cream puffin.

Why do birds flock together at the seashore?
Because one good tern deserves another.

Which bird digs through the garbage?
The trash can-ary.

DUMMY: If you're so smart, tell me why the sky is blue.
BRAIN: Sure. It's sad because there's too much air pollution.

Sparrow tire: A small, brown bird's belly.

TONGUE TWISTER:

A two-toed turkey towed two tubs of tea. Where is the tea the two-toed turkey towed?
Tossed in the tunnel where the turkey's key can protect it from the tongue of the tea-tasting toad.

TREE'S COMPANY

What does a porcupine bring to a barbeque?
The prickles.

What part of the newspaper does a rabbit like to read?
Lettuce to the editor.

A book never written:
A Walk in the Woods
by M. I. Tyred

What kind of joke does a squirrel like best?
Acorn-y joke.

How did the hiker find the right path through the woods?
By trail and error.

A book never written:
Identifying Poisonous Snakes
by Doobie Careful

Why did the rabbit become a comedian?
Because he was always very bunny.

How do you know when a mole needs money?
He burrows from his friends.

Why do so many chipmunks become letter carriers?
Because they are born with pouches.

What mouse fell in the mud?
Ickey Mouse.

What is the badger's favorite book?
The Red Badger of Courage.

Elmer and Ashley were walking in the woods when they came upon an orange mushroom.

ELMER: Ashley, you took a course in mushroom identification. Is this good to eat?
ASHLEY: I wouldn't.
They came upon a brown mushroom.
ELMER: Is this one good to eat?
ASHLEY: I wouldn't.
They found a speckled mushroom.
ELMER: How about this one?
ASHLEY: I wouldn't.
ELMER: Well, which mushrooms would you eat?
ASHLEY: I wouldn't eat any of them. I hate mushrooms.

What did one acorn say to the other when they fell to the ground?
Don't worry. Everything will be oak-ay.

What do you get when you cross a mouse with a bear?
Minnie the Pooh.

PHIL: Why are you building a second tree-house way out on that limb?

BILL: Because I want a branch office.

Knock, knock.
Who's there?
Thistle.
Thistle who?
Thistle sting if I touch it.

What mouse is the leader of all mice?
The mice-president.

What does an opossum eat on his birthday?
An upside-down cake.

What do trees do when they go on vacation?
They pack their trunks.

A book never written:
The Dangers of Tree Climbing
by Lou Smy Balanz

Who eats cookies and lives in a monastery?
The chocolate chip-monk.

WET AND WILD

Who crawls, has scales, and lives in Emerald City?
The Lizard of Oz.

Knock, knock.
Who's there?
Canoe.
Canoe who?
Canoe help me get this boat out of the water?

Who's green, lives in the water, and wears a coonskin cap?
Davey Crocodile.

What has tentacles and appears in the ocean after September 30th?
The Octoberpus.

What animal comes after the beagle?
The cee-gull.

A book never written:
River Rafting
by Flo Ting Along

What do baby porpoises play with?
Their doll fins.

Who is the eight-armed outlaw of the sea?
Billy the Squid.

How do whales wash their dirty clothes?
In the Tide.

Bassball: A sport for fish.

What snake discovered the Pacific Ocean?
Balboa Constrictor.

What has big claws, lives in the ocean, and works on science experiments?
A labster.

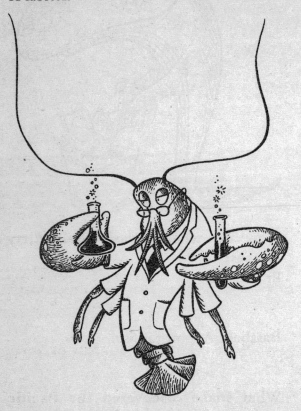

Knock, knock.
Who's there?
Giraffe.
Giraffe who?
Giraffe turned over and we fell into the lake.

What fish hums the second note of the musical scale?
The sting-re.

Knock, knock.
Who's there?
Otter.
Otter who?
Otter you learn to swim or you drown.

What sea creature goes great between two pieces of bread?
The peanut butter and jellyfish.

A book never written:
Down Niagara Falls
by Inna Barrel

What animal is good at licking envelopes?
The seal.

What does seaweed yell when it's in trouble?
"Kelp, kelp!"

Knock, knock.
Who's there?
Eyesore.
Eyesore who?
Eyesore someone dump garbage in the lake.

Where does a turtle keep his books?
On his bookshell.

Why couldn't the porpoise say the alphabet?

Because she always got lost at c.

How do fish build playgrounds?
They use their sea-saws.

Why did the octopus get arrested?
Because he committed armed robbery.

Who's the biggest nerd of the sea?
Moby Geek.

TONGUE TWISTER:

The swirling surf where Sylvia swam swept
Sylvia out to sea.

NATURAL NONSENSE

What cat holds up a building?
A cat-er-pillar.

The Braidy Bunch: Bananas with pigtails.

How did Mother Nature tell the forest that summer was over?
"Well, my dears, it's time to be leafing."

Why is a beaver a popular storyteller?
Because she always has a good tale.

How is a bump in a car door like a rat?
It's a road dent.

What is a calf's favorite searching game?
Cowhide and seek.

What should you do when a snake sticks out his tongue?
Tell him he's impolite.

What is part pig and part tree?
Porky pine.

What do we need to clean up outer space?
Comet.

What's the difference between a cobra having a good time and a tanning salon?
One is snake fun and the other is fake sun.

What happens when a sheep loses his coat?
He's cold.

Why was the greyhound embarrassed after he ran the marathon?
Because when he caught his breath, he lost his pants.

What dog stretches from one end of a bridge to the other?
The span-iel.

What makeup did the teenage wallaby wear on her first date?
Kangarouge.

A book never written:
Vegetable Gardening Is Wonderful!
by Rose Collard Glasses

Who is related to Mother Nature?
Her son, Flower.

What dog leads the cheers at football games?
The pom pomeranian.

How did the florist propose to his girlfriend?
He aster to marry him.

And how did his horse-loving girlfriend reply?
Neigh.

Hare cut: A rabbit's sore finger.

What loves a berry-filled cake, is tiny, and crawls on its belly?
The strawberry shortsnake.

Pop corn: Dad's bad jokes.

Why did the shrews call a taxi when their car broke down?
Because they needed a shrew driver.

What's brown, has whiskers, two tusks, and holds up the roof?
The wall-rus.

What's the difference between a cobra's puncture and a bakery?
One is a snake bite and the other is a bake site.